Paul Gardiner

A drummer's parlor stories

Paul Gardiner

A drummer's parlor stories

ISBN/EAN: 9783743342217

Manufactured in Europe, USA, Canada, Australia, Japa

Cover: Foto ©ninafisch / pixelio.de

Manufactured and distributed by brebook publishing software (www.brebook.com)

Paul Gardiner

A drummer's parlor stories

A DRUMMER'S PARLOR STORIES.

"'SPECIAL GUESTS OF THE PROPRIETOR.'
NO CHARGES"

Another Kind of Man. Page 57.

A Drummer's Parlor Stories

BY

Paul Gardiner

The Author of "Vacation Incidents," "Paul's Adventures To Date," and others.

ILLUSTRATED BY

E. J. READ

A. P. GARDINER
New York
1898

Copyright, 1898, by A. P. GARDINER.

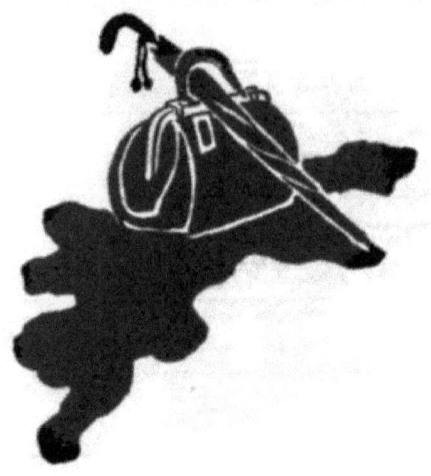

CONTENTS.

	Page
A RIDE WITH AN ARKANSAS PICNIC	13
MORNING OBSERVATIONS IN TAYLORVILLE	19
HELPING THE BRIDE ALONG	27

OVER DIAMOND JOE'S RAILROAD:

I.—THE MAN, BOB, I, AND THE "RAZOR BACK"	37
II.—BOB, I, AND ANOTHER MAN	45
III.—ANOTHER KIND OF A MAN	51

ON THE OTHER FELLOW'S TICKET	61
DEATH OF THE LOVED UNKNOWN	71

INTO THE MOONSHINE COUNTRY:

I.—I KICKED YOUR DOG	83
II.—A PIECE OF FRIENDLY ADVICE	93
III.—YOU MATCH ME	103

ILLUSTRATIONS.

	Page
	Frontispiece.
" 'Special guests of the proprietor.' No charges."	
The Arkansas Traveller	13
"So to the great amusement of the car I adopted temporarily, the orphan"	14
"We received in return a smile"	15
"I had left Bob asleep"	20
"On the 'Gossip's Bench'"	21
"It didn't work like his cob pipe"	23
"Bob wanted to pass the fan to the bride"	29
"'Now look here,' says Bob to me"	31
"Everything in readiness, we struck out for the city"	32
"'Gentlemen, you might find it more comfortable sitting on my veranda'"	38
"The 'razor back' winked the other eye when he saw us returning"	40
"'You just pick me out a box of the white ones'"	46
"With an inquiring smile, I said to Bob: 'It's ten per day, sure'"	53
"'Special guests of the proprietor.' No charges" (full page)	55
"Riding over and back we busied ourselves figuring out what our expenses would be"	56
"A visit down the street in Houston to some of the cut rate ticket brokers"	62
"I was to pass as a man with red hair, brown mustache and chin whiskers, a scar on the right cheek bone"	64

Page

"*I was gently assisted over the platforms and into the car*" (*full page*)	65
"*Bob's voice I could hear, as he told the conductor of the sick friend who occupied 'Lower Number Six'*"	67
"*They find themselves seated opposite each other at dinner table*"	73
"*There he stood in his long linen duster, hat in hand, smiling*"	75
"*He chewed the end of an unlit cigar, and was looking with a far-away, sad expression out of the window*"	77
"*To satisfy my wavering hopes, I read again and again the letter*"	85
"'*Want a hotel, young feller?*' *says he. 'Only one here'*"	87
"'*Now slope with me, young one!*'"	88
"*With a jerk of his thumb over his shoulder, the clerk indicated where the boss could be found*"	95
"*He was marking the retail prices upon the bottoms of the boxes*"	99
"*Looking at imaginary pictures on the walls, I leisurely sauntered out of sight of the hotel office*"	105
"'*It's heads—for a dollar*'"	106

A Ride with an Arkansas Picnic.

A Ride with an Arkansas Picnic.

TRAVELLING in Arkansas in the middle of July is not indulged in by non-residents of that part of the country for health or pleasure. It was the stern necessity to go where we could turn a dollar our way, which was chargeable to Bob Williamson and me being on the train which was to pick up a church picnic somewhere between Pine Bluff and Little Rock. The day was one of the hottest, and the dust fought with the soft coal cinders for the easiest lodging places upon our linen dusters. Bob and I occupied two seats, arranged facing each other. We buttoned our dusters up, and only for the rakish way in which our handkerchiefs were tied around our necks and the tilt of our soft felt hats, we might have been mistaken for a pair of native parish preachers. Perhaps the resemblance is what furnished the material for this sketch.

The Arkansas Traveller

We soon arrived at a small station where an unusual crowd of children, accompanied by their mothers, darky "mammies," and overgrown and underfed boys, were assembled. As soon as the train came to a standstill this motley array fiercely attacked the entrances. Bob held possession of our two seats until an appeal came before him in this way, which completely broke down his resolution. A woman came in carrying two urchins, apparently of the same age, herself weighing over two hundred pounds, with a good-natured face of ruby red, her hat pushed on one side, and she all but overcome with the heat.

"You are welcome to one of our seats," says Bob. In a minute we had our three new neighbors facing us on our extra seat. The extreme heat had made the children hard to manage, and the poor woman was exhausted.

"*So to the great amusement of the whole car I adopted, temporarily, the orphan.*"

"Let me have one of your children?" enquired Bob. Yes, she says, certainly, take this one. Bob played the role of indulgent father with such success that soon his charge was fast asleep in his arms. The mother, tired with the day's efforts and having perfect confidence in her newly made acquaintances, also goes peacefully to sleep. The remaining baby, left to fall from the arms of the helpless sleeper, is in imminent peril. I reasoned with myself thus, —if Bob had nerve enough to capture one of the twins while the mother was awake, I certainly am entitled to the other when I find it asleep and in danger. So to the great amusement of the whole car I adopted, temporarily, the orphan.

The mother slept peacefully on, dreaming of the "pink lemonade" and the "hot tomales" passed around at the picnic, 'til a rude call from the porter announcing the end of the ride for the Sunday School, the sleeping woman awoke startled.

With a Chesterfieldian bow we gave back the children and in return received a smile, which meant more from this grateful mother than the remark we often hear in higher society, "Oh, thank you, very kind of you I am sure."

" We received in return a smile."

I saw him in a lonely room,
   A-pacing to and fro;
His step was hurried and he paused
   From time to time in woe.

      His face was buried in his hands,
         His tears fell thick and fast;
      "Oh, from these tortured eyes," cried he,
         "Has peace forever passed?"

I shared his grief: the poignant words
   Came sobbing from his heart,
And so I tried with sympathy
   Some solace to impart.

      But all he said was, "Ne'er like me
         May you make this avowal—
      I've washed my face with yellow soap
         And cannot find a towel!"

Morning Observations in Taylorville.

Morning Observations in Taylorville.

I WAS prompted by one of those stray ideas that carelessly wander through your mind at times, feeling perfectly safe that they will never be detained, because of the indifference or inability of the possessor of that mind to catch on to a "good thing." This particular idea was to get up early, and board a morning train which passed through Decatur at sunrise on its way to St. Louis, and get off at Taylorville, a distance of about thirty miles down the road. I could then, after waiting two hours for the business part of the town to awaken, have an hour in which to pass the time with the unsuspecting (?) merchants, and incidentally have them admit, after a careful manipulation of the conversation, that they needed something in my line.

I had left Bob asleep, but he was carrying on an animated controversy with a couple of persistent flies, who always insist that "drummers" are entitled to all there is to be had for their money at cheap hotels. I left word at the office that, as a penalty for his not being wakeful and attentive to business, he could pay my bills and carry my baggage to the depot, and I would be on the train we had planned to take the night before, which would leave Decatur at ten o'clock in the morning.

"*I had left Bob asleep.*"

Walking from the station, which was an eighth of a mile outside of the town of Taylorville, that lovely Summer's morning, with nobody to talk to nor any noise to disturb me, it seemed a good chance to observe things. The first observation was that the sun was up just far enough to show the sparkling of the dew on the broad leaves of corn which could be seen for miles around the town. Corn raising was the industry in that section. The people you met talked about corn, they lived on corn, and corn growing was their only business. And thus it was when a new-comer pranced into town at that time of morning in the corn growing season carrying an indisputable air and manner about him that plainly said, "Well! the whole country is not engaged in corn raising," that three of the "oldest citizens" were surprised on the "gossip's bench."

Taylorville was then composed of one principal square, having one-story buildings fronting on all sides. The centre of the square is used for an open market-place and hitching posts for farm teams.

Sitting in front of one of these buildings,

"On the 'Gossip's Bench.'"

which had a lean-to roof as an awning over the sidewalk, were three typical old characters of that region; one chewed the end of a straw, one whittled a stick, and all three wore the same style of clothing, cut from the bolt of blue jeans at the corner store. All three were tall, thin, and sat with the grapevine twist to their legs.

"Good morning, gentlemen," I said, as I walked briskly up to them. "Could you tell me where I can find the hotel?"

Each looked at the other, one made as though to speak, then the third man said:

"You might try over thar."

I hurried over the street and found what served as a hotel. Leaving my order for a breakfast of ham and eggs, (the standing order when in doubt as to the cuisine department), I sallied forth again, this time in search of a barber. Meeting my acquaintances once more, I inquired for the town barber. The spokesman this time untwined his legs, and giving me a look of curious interest, said:

"I think I kin show you."

"Come along," I said, "looks to be a fine day."

"Good growin' corn weather," says he.

Arriving at the door of the barber shop, I saw a case of cigars inside.

"Will you smoke, sir?" I inquired.

With a childish bashfulness he accepted the cigar, with a light, which I handed him.

Turning to prepare for the shave, I removed my coat, collar and tie. Then glancing back at my new found friend, I saw he was having trouble. The end of the cigar was all ablaze, but despite the tremendous efforts he made, no smoke was visible from the right end of the cigar. He had just discovered the "durn thing" didn't work like his cob pipe. I turned away to hide my amusement—he had failed to bite off the end of the cigar. I saw in the mirror that he, thinking no one was looking, quickly stumped out the fire, placed the cigar carefully in the pocket of his blue jean trousers and hurried out to investigate further while hoeing among the rows of corn, promising himself never to let another newcomer disturb his peaceful thoughts.

"It didn't work like his cob pipe."

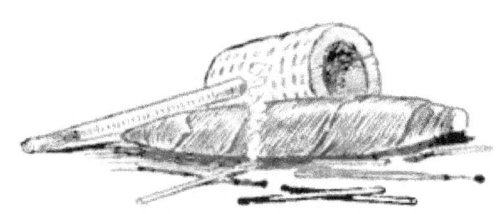

Helping the Bride Along.

Helping the Bride Along.

ONE of the incidents which become familiar to the constant traveller is the encountering of wedding parties, with the attendant "send off" by friends at the railroad stations, and the showers of rice thrown in at the windows upon the other passengers. Such experiences happening to the same persons at frequent intervals during a trip, are calculated to destroy the pretty romances and visions of cupids which flutter about the bridal pair. By the quick-eyed salesman, all the little ruses adopted by newly-wed couples to conceal from the travelling public their identity as bride and groom, are seen through at a glance.

On the occasion of which I write, it was not the customary tactics of wedding couples which interested Bob and myself, but rather the peculiarities of the groom, his dress, and more particularly, the attitude he assumed toward his bride and fellow passengers. His self-consciousness, and above all, his boorishness toward his pretty companion, were so apparent that the sympathies of the nearby passengers were soon enlisted with his "better half."

The groom (who, by the way, sat opposite us) evidently had a few points in mind which he felt necessary to impress upon the company. The first was that he had just been married, the second, that he had on his best clothes, and thirdly, he wanted no interference with his bride by outsiders.

It was this last named resolution that Bob "ran up against" principally, in his efforts to "help the bride along." He seemed to be one of those fellows who are unwilling to admit with an easy grace that the surroundings and situations are new to them and that they would be glad to receive any little suggestions or information to be had from their fellow travellers, but who rather assume an air of "knowing it all" which is a certain indication of ignorance.

As to the second point, it may first be remarked that June weddings in Arkansas might be more popular if the contracting parties would adopt a travelling trousseau suited to the demands of the climate. The middle of June down there is a warm time, and a favorite costume of the male sex, which allows for a certain amount of style and a whole lot of comfort, is made up of a black lustre coat, a pair of light-weight trousers, negligee shirt, low shoes and straw hat.

But as for our groom's attire, suffice it to say that he was done up in a very warm black, a rural high hat with a sack coat,

"*Bob wanted to pass the fan to the bride.*"

black kid gloves, a turn-down collar and a watch chain which would have done coupling service for the train.

After riding along for a half hour, the heat and dust in the car seemed almost unbearable, and our neighbor looked more aggressive each time we glanced his way.

Bob wielded a large sized palm-leaf fan, and having besides the proper kind of clothing for comfort, we seemed to get along very well. Bob wanted to pass the fan to the bride, but each time he looked her way he met the discouraging look of her "liege lord." Not to be baffled, at length he reached across the aisle and politely offered her the fan. As the groom was hesitating whether it might give him more trouble to accept it, the lady smiled and thanked him for his thoughtfulness.

We were proceeding along our way without further incident when suddenly the train came to an unexpected stop. Hurrying out, I found that the tracks ahead were blockaded by a freight wreck, and that we were three miles distant from Little Rock. A few enterprising cabbies had driven out from the city, and they were quickly appropriated by those in the forward cars.

We soon realized that we must get some conveyance to carry our sample trunks into town or the day would be entirely lost, our competitors thus gaining a day's lead on us. We were not in despair long, however, for not many moments later Bob espied approaching an old horse and weather-beaten wagon with a colored driver. Swooping down on the inoffensive old nigger, we took possession of his outfit. No argument was made over the price, nor did we tell what we wanted the rig for. I drove the wagon up to the end of the train

HELPING THE BRIDE ALONG.

where the baggage-car stood, and together we hustled our trunks in.

We had just turned about to make the start for Little Rock and the hotel, when

"'Now look here,' says Bob to me."

there beside the wreck we beheld a picture of helplessness,—the bride and her "Jonah," the groom.

"Now look here," says Bob to me, "I don't think it right to leave this poor girl

"*Everything in readiness, we struck out for the city.*"

Singing through the forests,
   Rattling over ridges;
Shooting under arches,
   Rumbling over bridges;
Whizzing through the mountains,
   Buzzing o'er the vale,—
Bless me! this is pleasant,
   Riding on the rail!

          Men of different "stations"
             In the eye of fame,
          Here are very quickly
             Coming to the same;
          High and lowly people,
             Birds of every feather,
          On a common level,
             Travelling together.

                    —*John G. Saxe.*

out here with that 'chump' of a husband. If we do she will have to lead him all the way to town afoot." So throwing aside further ceremony, Bob goes up to the couple and sharply demands from the fellow the check for their trunk.

Two valises comprised their baggage, and our colored man placed them in the wagon. Bob, meanwhile, gallantly helped the bride over the wheel and seated her upon the sample trunk, the groom still sullenly acting as though things should be different, but not even removing his black kid gloves to help load the baggage. Everything in readiness, we struck out for the city.

After we had gone about two miles, we came across the street-car track. Seeing in the distance a mule-car approaching, we then suggested to the bride that perhaps it would be pleasanter for her to take the groom aboard the car, and we would guarantee the safe delivery of the valises at the hotel if she could look after her husband.

Over Diamond Joe's Railroad.

I.—The Man, Bob, I, and the "Razor Back."
II. Bob, I, and Another Man.
III.—Another Kind of a Man.

The Man, Bob, I, and the "Razor Back."

WE had spent several weeks in Arkansas travelling aimlessly about, only now and then making a sale of goods. It was very necessary to procure some orders to accompany the frequent requests we made on our firms for remittances to pay our daily expenses. The orders themselves (needless to say) were never very large; but the promises for better results, should we be allowed to come again, were of a very roseate hue.

Before leaving the scenes of our late exploits, we were desirous of visiting the one place of interest which takes rank far and above anything else in the state, or in fact the whole United States. It is known as the Monte Carlo of America,—the Mecca of the gambler, the retreat of the invalid,

"Gentlemen, you might find it more comfortable sitting on my veranda."

and the delight of the pleasure tourist—the Hot Springs of Arkansas.

Malvern Junction is the name of the station where Diamond Joe's narrow gauge railroad emerges from the grim mountain defiles and connects with the Iron Mountain R. R. system. Here is where our experiences began as tourists for pleasure. We had about an hour to wait before the train of narrowly-built cars would leave to take us through the rocky passes to Hot Springs. We loitered about the station, looking at the axle grease frying in the Summer's sun on the car tracks, while the "razor back" hogs critically nosed our baggage on the platform.

Very soon we were approached by a man who looked not at all like the Mary's Little Lamb variety, but the soft gentleness of his voice as he volunteered a remark, was the cause for both a surprise and an uneasiness to us later on. He said:

"Gentlemen, you might find it more comfortable sitting on my veranda till the train arrives."

We looked across the tracks and saw a very unpretentious, low front, rough board structure, with a sign over the door which read, "Railroad Hotel." The stranger seeming so very kind, and we not being comfortable where we were, we took in the bait and strolled across.

We had no more than settled ourselves on his rough benches when a voice from the rear fell upon our unsuspecting ears so rough and full of ominous meaning that we looked up with a start to see who the ruffian might be. Imagine our surprise when standing over us, we recognized our solicitous friend of the lamb-like gentleness. He had announced that supper was ready and we had just ten minutes in which to eat it. There was no doubting his meaning,—it was simply this,—he wanted a dollar apiece out of us! I looked at Bob, he looked at the man, then both of us started

"Th 'razor back' winked the other eye when he saw us returning."

for the dining-room. Nothing was said and a very little was eaten. We paid over the money without even the privilege of registering a single objection, then calmly walked back again across the tracks to the railroad platform. I knocked my fist against the open palm of my other hand, Bob showed his white teeth, and the "razor back" winked the other eye as he saw us returning.

II.
Bob, I, and Another Man.

Bob, I, and Another Man.

AFTER gathering together our shattered courage and seeing our baggage put aboard the train, the start was made for Hot Springs. Some young sports of the neighborhood stood on the platform of the car and discharged their revolvers at whatever chanced to take their fancy, so that from the beginning of this short ride events of interest followed one another in quick succession.

Bob and I were conversing in whispers over our treatment at the hands of the hotel-keeper at Malvern Junction and wondering what would be the nature of the next experience, when we became conscious that somebody was standing at our side awaiting recognition. Looking up, we saw a large man with a flowing black beard, wide-rimmed felt hat, broad shouldered, and wearing a pair of blue goggles.

But for a sign hanging across his breast which read, "Help the Blind," we might have taken him for a prosperous native Arkansan. A large tray hung suspended by a strap around his neck, containing several small crates of long blackberries. He edged his way into our cross-seat, sat himself

"*You just pick me out a box of the white ones.*"

down comfortably, and immediately began to talk to us in an interesting manner, knowing apparently our vocation in life, and the section of the country from which we came.

Bob, whose suspicions had been aroused by the recent happenings, did not intend this time to be so easily worked for "a tenderfoot," so he ventured the query, "Selling berries?"

"Yes; won't you buy a box? They are fresh," he suavely replied.

There were boxes of blacks and other boxes mixed with white blackberries.

"Are the blacks and whites the same price?" says Bob.

"Yes, the same price, stranger," said he.

"Well," answered Bob, "you just pick me out a box of the white ones while I hunt for my change."

The trick was superbly worked. The fake "blind man" quickly selected the box of white blackberries from his tray, but just as quickly discovered the trap he had fallen into. Just then the train pulled into Hot Springs, thus saving the "sharp" any further embarrassment. On inquiry, we learned at the station that this *poor blind man* was the most successful "bunco steerer" and gambler in the town.

III.
Another Kind of a Man.

Another Kind of a Man.

THE adventures we had met with since we started on our little pleasure trip were not calculated to inspire a great amount of confidence in the acquaintances we were making in that particular section, and thus it happened when Bob was approached in a familiar manner by a gentleman who said that he hailed from the same town as he did, back in Ohio, that he was inclined to resent his advances.

This gentleman informed us that he was the proprietor of one of the best hotels in the place and that for old acquaintance sake he would be pleased to entertain us during our stay at Hot Springs. We hesitated before accepting the invitation, both of us thinking very hard of what dangers, if any, we would be subjected to should we accept. Knowing that we would be as safe in one hotel as another, however, we decided to take our chances with Bob's friend.

Our hand bags were taken in charge by the 'bus man, who drove us rapidly to the large and prosperous looking hotel of which Bob's acquaintance was the proprietor. The sumptuous offices and luxuriously furnished parlors which were visible from the clerk's desk, at which we were writing our names upon the register, had a panicky effect upon our spirits. I myself thought I could see five dollars per day, easily, charged for our accommodations, even though we might secure the lowest priced apartments.

The clerk received a word of instruction from his employer which was sufficient to start us immediately toward the rooms assigned to us upon the second floor. We were not held with the other arrivals to await the pleasure of the room clerk magnate.

We were shown up to two of the best rooms in the house. The inviting enameled bath tubs, soft carpeted floors, the immaculately white linen which covered the double beds, and the bevelled French plate mirrors that reflected our full-sized figures, caught our attention in a second of time.

We dismissed the colored porter, with a liberal tip. His manner toward us had very plainly indicated that no one who could be so rash as to engage those particular rooms would dare to bow him out with a smile and a promise.

The door closed, we each turned and silently walked toward the centre of the room. My hands were pushed down deep into my trouser pockets. It was very evi-

"With an inquiring smile, I said to Bob:—'It's ten p r day, sure.'"

dent that we were not in any easy state of mind. With an inquiring smile, I said to Bob:—

"It's ten per day, sure."

"Well, don't it look to be cheap even at that?" said he. "We will have money some day, and I intend to make these people around this place think we have plenty of the 'golden clinkers' right now."

Our rooms were sumptuously furnished—such elegance we had not been accustomed to for weeks. Comparing our appearance to the furnishings of our quarters, it would be very apparent that we were either a couple of foreign aristocrats travelling in disguise, or by accident had gotten into the wrong place. Hurriedly travelling from place to place, putting up with poor hotel accommodations, suffering all kinds of discomforts from the intense heat, it is not to be wondered at that we should have lost considerable in personal attractiveness. The large mirrors showed our full figures. Our alpaca coats, once black, were now a sunburnt brown and badly wrinkled, trousers bagged at the knees, linen soiled, while our straw hats would be rejected at a Bowery cleaning establishment.

Our pride was touched. We recalled that at home we enjoyed a reputation of being among the first to "catch on" to the new fads in men's attire as they came out. And why shouldn't we occupy fine apartments? We were just as nice people, if they only knew it, as any who came to that hotel, and thus we argued. Like a man whistling while going through a graveyard at night—he wasn't scared at all—oh, no! The same with us, as we speculated on the price of the rooms. We weren't scared. Uneasy though—just a bit nervous.

Our trunks by this time had reached the rooms, and we immediately began to renew acquaintance with our wardrobe.

ANOTHER KIND OF A MAN.

"'Special guests of the proprietor.' No charges."

The balance of the evening, before the eight o'clock dinner, we spent very creditably to ourselves, and after we had been seated in the dining-room a rapid survey of the guests was made. After which Bob remarked, as he squared his shoulders and stuck out his chest:

"Come, old pal, you flap your wings and crow, or else I will."

"Riding over and back we busied ourselves figuring out what our expenses would be."

The next morning being Sunday, we were offered the private horse and carriage of the proprietor, to take a drive over to the adjoining springs, a distance of five miles each way. Riding over and back we busied ourselves figuring out what our expenses would be, provided our invitation was of the same nature as those we already had extended to us during the past twenty-four hours. As worrying over the matter would not allow us to enjoy our beautiful and luxurious surroundings, we decided to leave ourselves in the hands of our friends or enemies, whichever they might prove to be, and settle up accordingly.

Monday morning came all too soon. We had enjoyed ourselves immensely. As we came up to the office desk of the hotel prepared to settle up, we were informed by the polite clerk, whose face wore a broad grin, that we were entered on the books as "special guests of the proprietor." No charges.

On the Other Fellow's Ticket.

On the Other Fellow's Ticket.

VERY often, in Texas, the situation presents itself disagreeably before the commercial traveller in this form: that his railroad fare from place to place is exceeding the profits on sales. It is then that the spirit of economy seizes hold upon the troubled salesman, and he looks about him for the first opportunity to cut down expenses. Hotel charges, Pulman car luxuries and the railroad ticket, each now comes in for a turn in this painful process.

Such was the predicament of Bob and me when, after several weeks of light business in the state, with our daily expenses running high, we found ourselves in a state of mind where we were inclined to take desperate chances.

The daily train over the Sunset Route from San Antonio arrived in Houston at six o'clock in the evening. Stopping there for supper and a change of engines it then hastens on its way to New Orleans.

Bob and I had figured up our expenditures for Galveston and Houston, consisting of our hotel accommodations, together with a few souvenirs we had purchased at the beach in Galveston, and we found that we had cash in hand, just enough to buy one straight ticket to New Orleans. To many, this would have been a rather awkward position to be placed in, but we did not see it in that way. We both had our watches with us, and there was no reason why they should not travel with a "C. O. D." tag attached to them, forward in the express car, as they had often done before, while their owners lounged in the parlor car assuming the air of an Eastern capitalist.

"A visit down the street in Houston to some of the cut rate ticket brokers."

Bob was a man who believed in having several cards to play. The watches were the last card played in all cases. A visit down the street in Houston to some of the cut rate ticket brokers left Bob in possession of two tickets. They read originally from El Paso to New Orleans, the coupon calling for the distance between El Paso and Houston having already been used and detached, and the time limit expired on the following day.

This limit as to time was not the only objection or undesirability of the "job lot" of transportation Bob had secured. They each had carefully written upon them a detailed description of the original buyers, who had signed an agreement with the railroad company that, on account of the reduced price under which they were sold, they could only be used by the original purchaser, etc.

The points of identification on one of the tickets would allow Bob to pass on it without creating any suspicions as to his not being the original purchaser.

As I read over the description on my ticket of the man whom I was supposed to represent, I was prepared to meet, to a reasonable limit, any little defects nature had overlooked in my make up which would allow me to pass as the average commonplace traveller, but the marks of recognition its first owner set down there on that ticket was a picture in "black and white" which very few of our later day artists would even attempt to draw, certainly much less attempt to impersonate.

I asked Bob if he had read my description.

"Of course not," said he, "the price is all

that I was interested in. Didn't I get the two tickets for the price of one? All the rest will be easy enough—just bluff it through, old man. What do you care whether he had red hair or not?"

It then dawned upon me that Bob was fully acquainted with the undertaking I had on hand.

I was to pass on the trip as a man over the usual height, with red hair, brown mustache and chin whiskers, a scar on the right

"*I was to pass as a man with red hair, brown mustache and chin whiskers, a scar on the right cheekbone.*"

cheek bone, and weighing one hundred and thirty-eight pounds. The inventory of my own appearance, if correctly taken, would read:—height five feet eleven inches, black hair, black moustache, and weight, one hundred and sixty-five pounds.

Bob announced at this juncture in the proceedings that no comparisons would be allowed in this particular case. His contention was exactly this: that I had been ill for several days—in fact at that very minute I should be confined to my

"*I was gently assisted over the platforms and into the car.*"

room and bed, and a close watch kept over me. For the next twelve hours he, Bob, was to be my nurse and physician. After hearing my case so ably discussed, I began to think I really did need care as well as protection.

The time had arrived for the start to the train. Although it was understood that I was a very sick man, Bob insisted that I was to carry my share of the hand bags as far as the depot. My "little act" was to begin after our arrival at the station. Under Bob's direction the colored porters in charge of the car in which our berths were located, came hurriedly into the waiting-room, and seeing the helpless and woe-begone appearance I had "put up," immediately singled me out as the sick passenger in "Lower Number Six." I was gently assisted over the platforms and into the car, where Bob hurriedly got me into bed and out of sight of curious eyes.

The closeness and stuffiness of parlor car berths even under the most favorable conditions are bad, but think of being shut up in one with the temperature registering one hundred and ten degrees in the shade! But I was in for it and had to help Bob get me through. To make matters worse, we had been told that the ticket "spotters" had just been over the road, and all conductors were on the "lookout."

The train was quickly speeding on its way toward New Orleans, with Bob on sentry duty outside my berth curtains. Now and then in answer to my questions as to how long he expected me to roast in that oven, he would gruffly command me to "get back into your cage there and shut up," or to "forget the heat" or "duck your head there, old chap."

Presently there came a sound to my ears

"Bob's voice I could hear, as he told the conductor of the sick friend who occupied 'Lower Number Six.'"

which, from the earnestness of the tones of the voices, warned me that my case was up before the conductor. Bob's voice I could hear, above the roar of the car, as he told the conductor of the sick friend who occupied "Lower Number Six," whose ticket he could present with his own, and would he be kind enough to allow the porter to help him safely carry his friend to a comfortable conveyance when we reached New Orleans.

The conductor said he would do all in his power to make the sick man comfortable, and he would also telegraph ahead to the company to have, when the train reached our destination, one of the invalid rolling chairs meet the car.

As soon as the sound of the voices died away, I got out from under the covers, just in time to meet Bob's grinning face pushed in between the curtains. All he said was —"Say Pop, you owe me the price of a ticket from Houston to New Orleans."

Death of the Loved Unknown.

Death of the Loved Unknown.

THE friendships and acquaintances existing among the travelling salesmen are interesting and remarkable in many ways. The formality of an introduction is very seldom resorted to, and oftentimes acquaintances are kept up for several years without either knowing the other's name, greeting when they meet with, say," Hello, there, 'Hardware!'"or "How-de-do, 'Collars and Cuffs,' I haven't run across you in a year!"—and if the routes of each be in a different direction it may be another year before these particular two meet again.

It may be, though, in three months that they find themselves seated opposite each other at dinner table in some hotel or railroad-eating house. Then a cordial greeting again is exchanged, an inquiry as to business may be passed, and good wishes extended on each side for future success.

No particular inquiry has been made as to what city each hailed from originally, or what either's name might be, yet a friendship is developing. During the intervening time both have been successful in standing the severe test of success "on the road," and unconsciously one finds a place in the heart and estimation of the other. Possibly if chance throws them together again they may be guilty of the pastime of exchanging names.

My readers, then, can readily understand how it could be that, on one of the Southern circuit trips of our party of eight salesmen whom (outside of Bob and myself) chance and amiability had brought together, we could be thoroughly well acquainted without knowing the full names of each individual.

Billie Robinson, who sold fine jewelery, was known as "Billie the Pearl," and when the sad misfortune which snatched poor Billie from our very arms into eternity, overtook our little band of big-hearted, congenial comrades, no casual observer could fail to feel that the death of the "Loved Unknown" was mourned with a silent grief only possible among broadminded, tender-hearted, charitable fellows.

Billie had become a general favorite. Unassuming, retiring in his manner, gentlemanly and kind, he always had a pleasant smile and a cheering word for us all. We all liked Billie.

Many might wonder how a person of his description could succeed in the capacity of salesman "on the road," but a close ob-

"They find themselves seated opposite each other at dinner table."

server of character could easily explain the secret of his success. It was in his conscientious work. He believed his firm manufactured the best jewelery on the market; they had entrusted him with the sale of it, and his convictions coupled with his courage and natural talents had made him a success in his business and a man beloved by his companions.

It was in Memphis, Tennessee, in the latter part of June, our little party of tourists was to meet at the six o'clock evening train on a large float guided by two powerful tugs which crossed the Mississippi River to the Arkansas side. The river at this point is several miles wide, and during high tide the current is swift and dangerous.

It was Billie's turn to do "satchel duty"—i. e., to see that the hand baggage of each in the company had been brought from the depot to the hotel and put aboard the train. This arrangement gave every saleman (except the one on duty) a chance to give the full time to business, catching the train from whatever point in the city he chanced to be in.

On this fateful evening three of the passenger coaches were detached from the train and backed down upon one of the tracks on the float. Billie, with the handbags, was forward in the coach which was coupled with the smoker and baggage car still upon the main line. Before his section of the train was sent down upon the launch, we had all stepped off the car platform of our train section upon the deck, and stood commenting upon the swollen and dangerous appearance of the river as, filled with logs and driftwood from up the country, it swept angrily past.

We were warned of the approach of the second section of our train by Billie, who shouted from the rear platform, "Out of the way, fellows, and give the expressman a chance." We all looked up in admiration of our favorite. There he stood in his long linen duster, hat in hand, smiling and

"There he stood in his long linen duster, hat in hand, smiling"

totally oblivious, like ourselves, of the danger he was in.

He stood sidewise to us and opposite the opening in the railing on the middle of the car platform. The brakes did not seem to respond to the efforts of the brakeman, and the cars still went on with an unlessened speed as they neared the bumper at the end of the track on the float.

Poor Billie! Before he could grasp the situation, or we utter a warning, the crash of the collision occurred, and we saw him, losing his balance, pitched headlong into the raging stream.

With a cry of horror we rushed to the edge of the boat; two of us flung off coats and hats, prepared for a plunge should he come to the surface, but we were disappointed even in that.

A small boat pushed out immediately from lower down stream, but the body of Billie was never recovered. It was supposed that he either became entangled in the wet folds of his expansive linen duster or that in his fall had struck headforemost against one of the floating logs which filled the stream, and never came to the surface.

The officials held the train until all hope of immediate recovery of the body was gone, then we pushed out for our next stop, Pine Bluffs, Arkansas.

The situation was a sad and an awkward one. A devoted companion had gone from us, a business firm had lost a valuable representative, and a sample case filled with costly jewelery had no owner nearer than—we did not know where.

It dawned upon our little band of mourners that we had some sacred duties to perform. The first question asked was, "Where did Billlie travel from?" We all knew in a general way that he represented a large firm in an Eastern city, but none knew where, definitely.

Another curious fact also developed,— Billie's full name was not known to any of the party, and neither had we heard him say anything about his family or domestic affairs. We all knew and felt this, how-

"He chewed the end of an unlit cigar, and was looking with a far away, sad expression out of the window."

ever—that away back in his home, wherever it might be, the news of his death would pain the hearts of many loved ones and admiring friends.

None of our party seemed willing to assume the lead in the investigation of Billie's effects, to ascertain the facts in regard to his identity—which it was necessary for us to know before we reached the next telegraph station, in order to notify the authorities in Memphis, and also to communicate with his home.

It was remarkable to see the varied ways in which Billie's death showed its effect upon the different temperaments of our company. Under ordinary circumstances, there were men among us who were given the preference, undisputed, in conversation, in their judgment upon daily questions arising in connection with our business pursuits and any discussions which might come up. From these men it was natural for the rest of us to expect that in a time like the present they would be the active and competent advisers. Rough in their dealings with men, uncouth in manner, and unaccustomed to the refining influences which surround many in different circumstances, it might be thought that grief would tap but lightly, if at all, at the door leading to their emotions.

Gathered in the smoking-car in seats facing each other, an observer would have noted among the rest, a muscular, brown-visaged man, the deeply furrowed lines in his cheeks telling of years of contact with the hard and relentless world, successes and failures holding about an even balance in the scales of fortune. He chewed the end of an unlit cigar and was looking with a far-away, sad expression on his face, out of the rapidly moving car window.

If you watched him closely you would frequently see a rapid succession of quivering winks of the eyelids. His silence was an unconscious act, his meditation was a sacred tribute to the present. We knew at once our comrade opposite was thinking, not only of the death of Billie, but of some shattered dream of happiness in his own life.

As soon as he realized that we had all silently chosen that he should be the one to proceed with the opening of Billie's grip, to see if we could find any information about his home, he turned to us and said:

"Boys, Billie is buried in the same grave that buried my only son, Tom, ten years ago. A hasty message was sent by his comrades to mother and me at Harrisburg, Pa. It was short and true—but too short and too true.

"We will tell them at home that Billie has gone on a long trip, that he won't be back for the Christmas holidays, for where he has gone, there diamonds and pearls do not need to be bought or sold. We will tell them that Billie has reached that land, of which it is written,—'The foundations of the wall of the city are garnished with all manner of precious stones . . . and every several gate is of one pearl: and the street of the city is pure gold, as it were transparent glass.'"

DON'T STOP AT THE STATION DESPAIR.

BY JOAQUIN MILLER.

We must trust the Conductor most surely;
   Why, millions on millions before
Have made this same journey securely
   And come to that ultimate shore.
And we, we will reach it in season;
   And ah, what a welcome is there!
Reflect, then, how out of all reason
   To stop at the station Despair.

Aye, midnights and many a potion
   Of little black water have we
As we journey from ocean to ocean—
   From sea unto ultimate sea—
To that deep sea of seas, and all silence
   Of passion, concern, and of care—
That vast sea of Eden-set islands—
   Don't stop at the station Despair!

Go forward, whatever may follow;
   Go forward, friend-led or alone.
Ah, me, to leap off in some hollow
   Or fen, in the night and unknown—
Leap off like a thief; try to hide you
   From angels, all waiting you there!
Go forward! whatever betide you
   Don't stop at the station Despair!

Into the Moonshine Country.

    I.—I Kicked Your Dog.
    II.—A Piece of Friendly Advice.
    III.—You Match Me.

I Kicked Your Dog.

TALES of lawlessness and a total disregard of the civilizing influences which go hand in hand with a higher education in the thickly populated parts of the States, frequently reach us through newspaper reports from certain sections of our resourceful country. Eastern Tennessee, parts of West Virginia, eastern Kentucky, and in fact, remote sections of almost every state, all have their "black sheep" corner.

It fell to my lot early in my travelling career to visit a section of the State of Kentucky, at the mouth of the Big Sandy River, where, at the present writing, many an older and seasoned traveller might well hesitate to venture.

Cattletsburg, a town of a few hundred inhabitants, lines the bank of the Ohio a a distance of several blocks. It enjoyed the distinction of being the headquarters of the raftsmen coming down the Big Sandy to form a junction with the Ohio River. It was also the market-place for the illicit corn whiskey distilled in the mountains by the enterprising mountaineers, whose almost inaccessible domain this uncertain river traversed. The stills, hidden under crags and side hills, the locations of which were known only to the owners and a trusted member of the family, were objects of the most desperate and daring research made by the state officials, the hated sheriffs.

Cattletsburg, although small and insignificant in itself, as compared with other business centres in different parts of the state, contained one large and prosperous general store. The firm with whom I was engaged had long desired to have a line of goods which they manufactured, introduced for sale into that section of the country through this particular merchant. Either the former representatives of my firm had refused to risk their destinies by boldly walking into the very haunts of the enemies of reciprocity and intercourse with the outside world, or else I was selected as the one, who, from a youthful, inoffensive and non-combative appearance, was the least calculated to be taken as an accomplice of the government deputies in search of "moonshine" evidence, or a sympathizer of the never ending

I KICKED YOUR DOG.

feuds of the Hatfields, McCoys or Masons

However it came about, I was told to go, and the same letter from my firm informed me that the merchant at Cattletsburg would be expecting me. Nothing better could have been said which would have had the effect in strengtnening my courage to go anywhere than that a

"To satisfy my wavering hopes, I read again and again the letter."

prominent merchant was "waiting 'til I came." My importance as a valuable man increased from that moment.

From Parkersburg, West Virginia, I travelled on the Ohio River Railroad toward Cattletsburg. En route I busied myself by re-arranging my samples, which I took out and returned again to my sample case, which lay open on the double seat before me, all the while building air castles of great deeds in large sales, "the loikes of such orders" my firm had never had sent them.

As time passed, I noticed, with an increasing concern, that the *tout ensemble* of the passengers in my coach had changed since leaving Parkersburg, and that at each station we stopped at as we neared my destination, I saw one after another of my original travelling companions leave the train, and those who took their places, to my way of thinking, did not inspire me with a desire to make any of their acquaintance. As the car began to fill up, I turned back the extra seat I had appropriated, and chose to hobnob with my sample case as a more agreeable and trusty companion than I had "sized up" the "shifty" looking lot of citizens to be who surrounded me.

I began to think that my train had crossed the border into some unfrequented and uninhabited country. In the places at which we stopped, nothing was to be seen in the way of busy streets and well kept lawns and fences, but on the contrary, to use a slang expression, things were "on the blink."

Railroad stations were uninviting. The name of the stop on the signboard could scarcely be read. Men stood about in slouched felt hats, their dirty jean trousers tucked into their boot tops, beards unkempt, round, stoop shouldered, their hands pushed down into their pockets, and as they rolled a tremendous quid of tobacco around in their mouths and slunked away with the passing of the train, I began to question the authenticity of my letter from the firm. To satisfy my wavering hopes, I read again and again the letter telling me to "go to Cattletsburg; they were waiting for me there."

The train passes in the rear of Cattletsburg at a distance of about a five minutes' walk. A wide cinder path leads up from the depot to the main street of the town. Alighting from the train with myself came the greater number of the passengers who occupied the car with me. As I walked along the platform using my regular tactics of following the crowd in a strange place, I came up to a muscular young fellow in charge of a large sized wheelbarrow.

"'Want a hotel, young fellow?' says he. 'Only one her...'"

"Want a hotel, young fellow?" says he. "Only one here. I will wheel her up (meaning my grip) for 'two bits.' I guess you'll come."

I did come, and was very glad to accept him as an escort.

The procession up to the town was an exciting one, and full of interest before we reached the hotel. The passengers walking toward the town had formed into three squads. Two separate squads of my fellow passengers of the "shifty" type were a little in advance of myself and the man who propelled the wheelbarrow.

"'Now slope with me, young one!'"

Just to be "in the swim," I suppose, and to lend a gist and finish to our advance on Cattletsburg, a shaggy, wet, ill-kept and faded yellow dog trotted in the line. Following the natural bent of their feelings, some fellow in the second group called out to the first lot of visitors:

"Hey, stranger, I kicked your dog."

One of the group addressed, replied, "'Taint my dog, no how."

"Wall, I'd a kicked him anyhow, if he were. Naow smoke that," says the first gent.

My man of the wheelbarrow turned to me, and in a tone of voice which meant immediate action, said quickly: "Those dubs mean to get acquainted, and there's going to be a 'mix' mighty soon. Now 'slope' with me, young one." And without waiting to see the "finish," I was landed hurriedly at the hotel, very glad to pay over the "two bits" for my safe delivery and that of my sample case.

(Continued in "A PIECE OF FRIENDLY ADVICE.")

II.
A Piece of Friendly Advice.

A Piece of Friendly Advice.

IT was about four o'clock in the evening of this misty November day when I inscribed my name upon the register of the City Hotel in Cattletsburg, and already the shades of darkness had added to the gloomy appearance presented by the dingy hotel, dilapidated sidewalks and the muddy street, which ran parallel with the river and was flanked by a single row of squatty and uneven buildings, which represented (with the single exception of the concern I had come to call upon) the business portion of the town.

I was no longer the confident and important personage I had figured myself to be earlier in the day. Somehow my hat seemed big for my head, and my waistcoat was too loose about the chest. I was in the town, though, where the merchant with a large and prosperous business was awaiting my coming. I had just re-read the letter from my firm, and was disgusted at myself for losing, for the time being, a proper self-appreciation. Getting out my business card and placing it in a convenient pocket, I set out with a renewed vigor to find my man.

This proved an easy task, for down at the end of the block, with the front of the building facing full up the street, stood a large, modern built, and well appointed store building. The sight of this had a tendency to revive in me an eagerness to "get at 'em" for the orders. Having filled out my waistcoat again to the full dimensions, and my hat being a better fit in consequence, I marched into the establishment with a stride, and a manner befitting my important mission and the commercial standing of the firm which I had the honor of representing.

I made inquiry as to the whereabouts of the proprietor, and with a jerk of his thumb over his shoulder, accompanied by a curious look, the clerk indicated where the boss could be found.

I went in the direction pointed out to me and found Mr. Carter, the proprietor, standing in the midst of several piles of hat boxes which hid him, except for his head and shoulders, from view. He was engaged in checking off the quantities from

A PIECE OF FRIENDLY ADVICE.

"With a jerk of his thumb over his shoulder, the clerk indicated where the boss could be found."

the bill he had received for his latest purchase, and was marking the retail prices upon the bottoms of the boxes.

Before I could speak, not knowing that he had noticed me, he addressed me thus:

"Howdy, Boy! Don't live in Kentucky I reckon Don't look like you come from up Cinc'nata way, nuther. Want to talk to me, son?"

The tone of Mr. Carter's voice reassured me. I produced my card and sailed in, first repeating that my firm had corresponded with him regarding my coming, and that I was prepared to quote prices and to book him ahead on the next season's styles.

Mr. Carter at first took on a look of surprise which soon changed to one of amusement, and cutting me short in my presentment of the case, expressed himself in these words:

"I don't know nuthin' 'bout this yere you been tellin' me. I reckon your people done made a mistake, for I didn't get no letter, sure 'nuf."

The look of deep disappointment and chagrin which, at this unexpected announcement, passed over my face, must have aroused the interest and sympathy of the merchant. Before I could recover myself from the paralyzing shock I had received, Mr. Carter turned to me, and in a kind, fatherly tone of voice, said:

"Son, I reckon you won't mind. I know these yere parts a heap. It will be powerful dark soon, and my advice is to git in under cover. These yere Big Sandy ''shiners' is 'bout lookin' for trouble, an' they might calklate gittin' reckless with you. Come back in the mornin' and tell me 'bout that letter your firm done send me."

Calling to one of the colored porters who stood near, he ordered him thus:

"It was marking the retail prices upon the bottoms of the boxes."

"Heah, nigger! Carry this gemman 'round to the hotel right quick. Now watch out for 'im."

I thanked him kindly, and wishing him a good night, hurried with my body guard back to the hotel.

That night, needless to say, I spent at home. I did not care to wander up and down the one street of the town, nor to stand on the banks of the Ohio, absently gazing at the slanting rays of the moonlight as it played on the yellow flabby wavelets caused by the uniting waters of the Big Sandy and Ohio.

The company I found indoors at the City Hotel were sufficiently interesting and entertaining in their way to influence me to remain under the protection of my friend of the wheelbarrow episode, who acted as my especial sponsor while I remained about the hotel.

After a comfortable night's rest and a calm review of the situation, I went around bright and early next morning to Mr. Carter's store. I found him in a very amiable mood, inclined to listen to what I had to say, and from an amused attitude at first, he fell into the interested state, and then to his own surprise and my apparent advantage, he began to buy from the samples of the lines of goods I had shown him, 'til his purchases amounted to a very respectable bill.

After the usual exchanges of invitations of a business nature, I returned to my hotel to await the next train which would carry me back from West Virginia soil to the land in God's country beyond the Big Sandy.

Upon the next trip of the Cincinnati drummer, who had been selling to the Cattletsburg firm for years, he found himself supplanted, and by a tenderfoot at that.

A PIECE OF FRIENDLY ADVICE.

The president of the company for whom I went with such great expectations to meet the merchant who was " waiting 'til I came," enjoys a good laugh even now when he recalls the successful ruse under which he placed Mr. Carter's name upon the books of his concern.

(Continued in " YOU MATCH ME.")

III.
You Match Me.

You Match Me.

MY success of the morning in the interest of my firm, coupled with the return of daylight, had revived within me a latent spirit of adventure and recklessness, which I possess to a mild degree under favorable conditions. I had six hours of a wait for the train which was to carry me away from the exciting and interesting scenes of the past twenty-four hours, back into the territory where I would quickly resume the humdrum even tenor of my way.

The night before the morning of which I write, I had spent observing the guests at the Cattletsburg City Hotel. Outside of myself, I think they were all residents of the town or of the nearby country, composed principally of raftsmen, boatmen, and mountaineers. The bar-room of the hotel and the office were the popular lounging places of the village, and thither came the sports, card players, checker players, crap shooters, and the penny matchers.

The spirit of gambling was developed to an amazing degree in Cattletsburg.

Several groups of men where engaged in what is commonly known as the innocent pastime of "matching pennies." I was attracted to a couple of the "matchers" who were seated at a small stand removed from the other players, and intensely engaged in carrying on a game which, if I had seen it at all in a section of the country north of the Mason & Dixon line, I would have passed by with the mental observation—a childish amusement only.

The expression on the faces of the two players at first interested me, and from my position seated by the wood-fire stove I moved nearer the players. Then I could hear these words pronounced in a monotonous tone, with a studied lack of expression or inflection of the voice, "Heads—Tails—Heads—Heads—Tails—Tails."

Occasionally the conversation between the contestants was varied by—"You match"—or "I raise you to a quarter." Each "matcher" had the privilege to call a change from a five-cent match to a ten-cent or a twenty-five cent match. Money was changing hands rapidly. No loud talking, laughing or hilarity of any kind, customary with games of chance, went with this duet of "matchers."

Although I had become interested in the game and fascinated by the nerve displayed by the players, an uncomfortable, uneasy feeling seized hold upon me. One of the young men, the son of the proprietor of the hotel, was steadily and surely adding to his pile of coin from that of his opposite.

And it was a speculation as to the events which might follow the finish of that pile that caused my alarm. I had learned thus quickly of the people of Cattletsburg that the master of an extensive vocabulary would not prevail against the argument of a self-cocking revolver. Besides, the merchant, Mr. Carter, (now my friend), had

"Looking at imaginary pictures on the walls, I leisurely sauntered out of sight of the hotel office."

told me to "git in under cover." So with a feigned air of being greatly bored with the "childish" amusement, I slid my hands into my trouser pockets, and looking at imaginary pictures on the walls, leisurley sauntered out of sight of the hotel office.

My peregrinations had brought me to the foot of the stairway (accidentally, of course), and without looking a farewell to the "penny matchers," I bounded up the stairs four steps at a time, and into my room out of harm's way.

I lay awake figuring the length of time it would take for the winning "matcher" to get the whole of the money of the loser till I fell into a sleep and dreams filled with noises of chinking money and exploding revolvers.

"'It's heads—for a dollar.'"

The next morning as I sat writing out my order which I had taken, to be forwarded to my concern, I had as my neighbor the successful winner of the matching game of the night before. As usual he was quiet, saying nothing to his companions, some of whom sat around the office. He was tilted back in the chair, his knees and chin keeping close company, a soft felt hat jammed down upon his head. Occasionally he straightened up and expectorated tobacco toward the box of sawdust in the middle of the floor which acted as a cuspidor.

While we were each pursuing his separate thoughts, a figure appeared in the doorway. I looked up suddenly and recognized the newcomer as the partner with the man at my side in the game of matching the night before. He was also recognized by my neighbor, but no indications of a greeting were made. Sullen and determined he looked, quietly and deliberately he walked up to his friend, drew a chair alongside, reached into his pocket, and slapped a coin down upon his knee, as he said:
" It's heads—for a dollar."
The son of the hotel keeper hesitated, looked once, and only once, at his victim of the night before.
He put down his dollar and uncovered: it was tails—he lost. Not a word was spoken by either. The visitor replaced the chair in the place from which he had taken it, took a fresh chew of tobacco, and sauntered off down the street.
The man at my elbow ventured no remarks. I knew that an expression of my sympathy would not be appreciated. So I did the only wise thing left for me to do—politely minded my own affairs.

www.ingramcontent.com/pod-product-compliance
Lightning Source LLC
Chambersburg PA
CBHW031407160426
43196CB00007B/933